Practising Your Faith

Understanding the Church's 5 Precepts

by
Fr Lewis Berry CO

*All booklets are published thanks to the
generous support of the members of the
Catholic Truth Society*

CATHOLIC TRUTH SOCIETY
PUBLISHERS TO THE HOLY SEE

Contents

All rights reserved. First published 2016 by The Incorporated Catholic Truth Society, 40-46 Harleyford Road London SE11 5AY Tel: 020 7640 0042 Fax: 020 7640 0046. © 2016 The Incorporated Catholic Truth Society.

ISBN 978 1 78469 104 2

A Journey through the Precepts

What are the precepts of the Church? This book focuses on a simple yet challenging element of the Catholic faith which it's important to know about and understand. The precepts take up just half a page of the *Catechism of the Catholic Church*, and yet, when we start to reflect on them, we find in them a "rule of life" for Catholics, a "game-plan" which directs us decisively on the path towards God and his salvation. The precepts were well-known to our parents and grandparents in recent times we've heard less about them. We're going to take a journey through the precepts, learn something of their history, and try to answer some questions we may have about them. But first, we need to ask - What are the precepts?

▶ What are the precepts?

The word "precept" comes from the Latin *praeceptum*, meaning a rule of order, a command, or law. Each of the five precepts in the *Catechism* (Nos. 2042-2043) is an important law of the Church which obliges you and me to do certain things. As we'll discover in this booklet, the discipline they give us - the rule they establish - deals with the most fundamental elements of Catholic life.

The first precept is: "You shall attend Mass on Sundays and holy days of obligation and rest from servile labour." This precept points to the supreme value of assisting at Mass each Sunday and holy day; it also tells us to rest, so as to hallow the Lord's day, most especially with our families.

The second is: "You shall confess your sins at least once a year", providing a minimum observance of the Sacrament of Reconciliation - a challenge to us if we've been putting off going to confession!

The third states: "You shall receive the sacrament of the Eucharist at least during the Easter season", pointing us to the loving Lord who desires to give us himself in Holy Communion, to which the Church therefore at least periodically obliges us.

The fourth is: "You shall observe the days of fasting and abstinence established by the Church." This binds us to limit how much food we eat on certain days of fasting (e.g. Ash Wednesday) and to abstain from meat on Fridays, reflecting the Gospel emphasis on penance as a way of uniting ourselves to the cross of Christ.

The fifth and final precept tells us: "You shall help to provide for the needs of the Church", requiring us to give - to the extent we are able - towards the material support of the Church, for her ministers, buildings, etc., and for the work of evangelisation.

▶ History of the precepts

From the earliest days of the Church, a need was felt to establish certain key points of conduct which the baptised were required to observe. We see this in the Scriptures themselves, whether it be regulations about abstaining from certain foods (cf. *Ac* 15:1-21) or the practice of common worship (cf. *Heb* 10:25). As the centuries went on, and some aspects of the Christian tradition needed to be re-emphasised, bishops composed lists of the most central aspects of Church discipline. We find in the *Penitentiary* of Theodore of Canterbury (in the 600s) and in the writings of Regino, Abbot of Prüm (d. 915) reference to the necessity of attending Mass each Sunday, on how Lent must be kept, and how frequently Catholic Christians should receive Holy Communion. As the medieval epoch reached its height, particular precepts started to be singled out as universally binding. Famous is the list of St Antoninus of Florence (1389-1459), who numbered ten such precepts, including the special observance of certain feast days and the practice of confession. It was at the time of the Catholic Reformation that the precepts started to look very similar to those we have today, with lists by St Robert Bellarmine (1542-1621) and St Peter Canisius (1521-1592) especially influential. For centuries there continued to be some variation between the precepts from place to place, but in modern times the Church has retained and established universally the five precepts found in the *Catechism*.

▶ Difficulties with the precepts

Are the precepts really still relevant today? Perhaps one reason why the precepts are not talked about much today is because they've attracted some negative connotations. Let's deal with three of these negative ideas in turn, because in doing so we can enter more fully into the true meaning and value of the precepts.

First: today, we feel that we don't like to be "*told what to do*". The precepts are commands, they are a kind of law, and they speak to us of our obligations. Isn't it better, we say, to go to Mass because we want to, rather than because there is a law telling us to do so? Isn't it better that we really feel the need to go to confession, rather than reading that we are obliged to whether we like it or not? Is Church law the best way to lead us to God?

We want to make mature choices in our religious life, as in everything else. We sense instinctively that to desire something and choose it freely is the most authentically human way of living. But don't we also recognise that, to choose what is best, we so often need guidance and support? Sometimes, what we might *want* - from a car we can't really afford, to a sexual encounter with someone we meet on the street - *isn't* what is truly right for us. The things the precepts speak of are the most valuable gifts God has given us. By going so far as to require us to make use of these gifts, the Church is showing us, with a kind of loving urgency, that it is these above all that we *should* want. If we tell ourselves that we don't need or want them, the Church, in the name of Christ, warns us that we deceive ourselves.

▶ True change of heart

A second point is linked to the first: we ask if the precepts can breed a certain *formalism* in our Catholic practice, as if being a Catholic were a matter of complying with certain rules of observance - what we eat, when we go to Church, etc. - but forgetting the priority of conversion, the call to "put off your old nature which belongs to your former manner of life and is corrupt…and be renewed in the spirit of your minds, and put on the new nature, created after the likeness of God" (*Ep* 4:22-23). Are we tempted to think that by fulfilling a few laws we will be saved, without a true *metanoia* (change of heart)? And so we could approach the fault of the Pharisees: "…you are like whitewashed tombs, which outwardly appear beautiful, but inside they are full of extortion and rapacity" (*Mt* 23:27).

Pope Francis has repeatedly drawn attention to the danger of a religion based on "regulations", "precepts" or "rules". For in this sense our religion is not a "religion of precepts": it is the renewal of our heart which, above everything else, God desires. And yet, how could we be changed, renewed, without responding to that call in specific gestures of faith and charity? Our faith is not a beautiful theory but a life-changing vocation which affects our actions as well as our thoughts. The precepts teach us the fundamental actions which define our lives as Christians; so they give us the means of conversion, the path we must travel if we desire to be changed, to be remade in Christ. Of course, the precepts teach us how to *start* on this path: the Church, as we'll explore in this book, then wishes to lead us ever deeper into prayer, self-denial and charity.

Thirdly, the precepts could be seen as a *burden*, stressing the obligations of the Gospel rather than the joy and hope that it brings into our lives. Here the words of Christ, again about the Pharisees, may resonate: "They bind heavy burdens, hard to bear, and lay them on men's shoulders"

(*Mt* 23:4). Do we or others want to feel weighed down by laws rather than knowing that Christ has set us free?

St Thomas Aquinas strikingly pointed out that the precepts which we have from Christ and the apostles "are very few". The Lord assured us that his yoke is easy and his burden light. The precepts of the Church, rather than imposing many or difficult practices, speak to us simply of the most essential observances of our faith. Do we view these minimum observances - what the Church puts forward as the "baseline" - as burdensome? If so, to reflect on the precepts of the Church - what they mean, what fruits they can bring, and where they are leading us - is an opportunity to rediscover that, far from burdening us, these are ways in which Christ, the Light of the World, sheds his light on us and fills us with his peace.

▶ The universal call to holiness

The Second Vatican Council's *Constitution on the Church* (*Lumen Gentium*) says: "The Lord Jesus, the divine teacher and model of all perfection, preached holiness of life to each and every one of his disciples of every condition. He himself stands as the author and consummator of this holiness of life: 'You, therefore, must be perfect, as your heavenly Father is perfect' (*Mt* 5:48)" (par. 40). In these words we find a central aspect - perhaps *the* central aspect - of the Council's message: the universal call to holiness. Holiness is not simply for people we've read about for priest, monks or nuns; holiness is for us - it's what we, above everything else, are called to. And if we wish to attain that goal, don't we ask that same question which the crowd, when they first heard the Gospel preached, asked St Peter and the apostles: "Brethren, what shall we do?" (*Ac* 3:37)? The Church, handing us the precepts, is insistent in her response: "do this and you will live" (*Lk* 10:28). So she reminds us of that "lifestyle" which has characterised believers of all times: as St Paul says, "you know how…we exhorted you and charged you to lead a life worthy of God, who calls you into his own kingdom and glory" (*1 Th* 1:10). And while the precepts are addressed to us individually, they call us to a continual growth in our communion with Christ in his Body, which is the Church, and to support each other on our Christian journey:

> "until we all attain to the unity of the faith and of the knowledge of the Son of God, to mature manhood, to the measure of the stature of the fulness of Christ… speaking the truth in love, we are to grow up in every way into him who is the head, into Christ" (*Ep* 4:13,15).

The First Precept:

"You shall attend Mass on Sundays and holy days of obligation and rest from servile labour"

Our Christian observance of "the Lord's Day" is rooted in the ancient faith of the Jews. A key feature of the Old Covenant is to "remember the Sabbath day to keep it holy" (*Ex* 20:8) - a day of worship and rest, reflecting God's "rest" after his work of creation (*Gn* 2:2-3). Christians, understanding the centre of their faith to be the death and resurrection of Jesus, from earliest times observed their new Sabbath on Sunday: its defining moment was the celebration of the Eucharist (see *Ac* 20:7). No surprise, then, that the vision of St John in the book of Revelation, a vision deeply linked to the Christian liturgy, occurred "on the Lord's Day" (*Rv* 1:10). Nor did the early Christians forget that this was the day of the sending of the Holy Spirit, the day of Pentecost. In a beautiful way the Church Fathers understood that this new Sabbath, Sunday, also represented the very beginning of God's creation in Genesis - both the day of the creation of the world, and of God's re-creation of it in Christ in the power of the Spirit. It was a conviction for which Christians were to pay, even with their lives. In times of persecution, when Christian assemblies were banned, Christians risked death to assist at Mass. When observance faltered, however, bishops and Church councils repeatedly re-emphasised the importance of what came to be called the "Sunday precept".

▶ When do I have to go to mass?

The first part of this precept speaks for itself. It requires a Catholic to be present at Mass each Sunday of the year, and also on certain holy days of obligation which fall during the week. In England and Wales, these are Christmas Day (25th December), and the feasts of Sts Peter and Paul (29th June), the Assumption of the Blessed Virgin Mary (15th August) and All Saints' Day (1st November). (If any of these last three feasts falls on Saturday or Monday it is transferred to the Sunday). Other countries have different days of obligation. The precept refers to attendance at Mass either on the Sunday or holy day itself, or on the previous evening (the "vigil" of the feast).

This precept - as for each of the precepts - does not bind us if we literally *cannot* fulfil it. This would include those who are ill or very infirm due to old age, those looking after young children, or someone undertaking necessary travel which truly impedes them from getting to Mass. Work may reasonably excuse someone, if his work is important to public order (e.g. a policeman), or if it represents the only possibility of earning a livelihood and his employer obliges him to work on Sunday. But even in these cases Catholics must fulfil the precept if they *can* find a way: by looking for a local Mass they can attend (e.g. on Saturday or Sunday evening) or by trying to arrange work so as to be free to get to Church. The precept doesn't ask the impossible: but it *does* require of us the possible. (The precept isn't fulfilled by attending a service in a non-Catholic Church, nor by participating in a Mass by television or radio).

▶ What is servile labour, and how do I rest from it?

The second part of the precept is sometimes overlooked. We're told that we should "rest from servile work". This originally referred to work done by serfs, work from which they were freed on Sunday and holy days. What does "servile work" mean for us today? Canon Law gives us a useful explanation, saying that we "are to abstain from those works and affairs which hinder the worship to be rendered to God, the joy proper to the Lord's day, or the suitable relaxation of mind and body". According to this definition, we judge "servile work" by how it affects us. Does a particular type of work stop us getting to Mass or devoting the time to prayer which we should on the "Lord's day"? Is it work that burdens and depresses us? And, last but not least, does it stop us having time for relaxation, and especially together with our families? Some forms of "work" are actually undertaken as forms of relaxation, such as gardening; others are necessary, such as cooking. But some things, like unnecessary housework or shopping, we shouldn't do on a Sunday. Nor should we forget that we can *cause* servile work for others: by regular Sunday shopping, for example, we are creating the demand which causes shops to employ more staff, staff who themselves are called to - and who need - the Sabbath rest. How can we help to create a society in which the Lord's day is honoured and loved by all?

▶ The joy of the sabbath rest

We see clearly in this precept how the Church, rather than encumbering us with unmanageable duties, is seeking to release us to worship God and share in the joy of the resurrection. We can be tempted to think that other things should take priority over attending Mass: taking children to sports matches, sleeping in, or visiting the shops. Yet Our Lord speaks to us as he spoke to those on the Mount: "Do not be anxious, saying, 'What shall we eat?' or 'What shall we drink?' or 'What shall we wear?'" (*Mt* 6:31) These things are all good things, but they cannot be set on a level with God himself. His Church, then, guiding us to see beyond passing things and to seek what endures, repeats the words of the Lord: "Seek first his kingdom and his righteousness, and all these things shall be yours as well" (*Mt* 6:33). Of course it is difficult to find time for everything: but the precept points to the truth that, if we find time for this, "the one thing necessary" (cf. *Lk* 10:42), God *will* bless us in countless other ways.

And so for the command to rest. Anyone knows that a workaholic sometimes needs to be told to relax. And so do we on Sundays: to arrange our time and our activities in such a way as to prioritise prayer, recreation, truly social opportunities that don't wear us out but rather refresh us, placing emphasis on what brings our families together. Funnily enough, sometimes it is we who burden ourselves

- by wanting to keep up with the neighbours, by spending money we don't have, or by starting arguments which make for a bad atmosphere. It's for these reasons that Pope St John Paul II so emphatically told us: "I would strongly urge everyone to rediscover Sunday: *Do not be afraid to give your time to Christ!* Yes, let us open our time to Christ, that he may cast light upon it and give it direction" (Apostolic Letter *Dies Domini*).

The Second Precept:
"You shall confess your sins at least once a year"

Confession is something very distinctive to our Catholic faith. When a priest or practising lay Catholic starts to make a non-Catholic friend, one of the first questions about the faith they are asked is usually about confession. What is the point of confession? Isn't it unreasonable to confess what you've done wrong - even things that no one else knows about - to another person? And where do you find it in the Bible?

▶ What is the point of confession?

The Sacrament of Penance - otherwise known as the Sacrament of Reconciliation or confession - has varied and developed in its form in the course of Christian history. Its roots, however, are profoundly biblical - indeed connected with the very heart of Christian revelation. "Receive the Holy Spirit. If you forgive the sins of any, they are forgiven; if you retain the sins of any, they are retained" (*Jn* 20:22-23). Catholics have always understood that these words of Our Lord to his apostles tell us that this sacrament is nothing less than a gift of Christ himself to the Church - and to each one of us. Whilst Baptism brings us into the friendship of Jesus Christ and forgives all our sins, confession, as the Fathers of the Church described it, is the "second plank [of salvation] after the shipwreck which is the loss of grace" (see the *Catechism of the Catholic Church* 1446). In other words, if we offend God by sin then he, like the father in the parable of the prodigal son, reaches out to us with his healing love, and restores us to himself.

The practice of individual confession developed more universally in the second Christian millennium, but an absolute constant in Catholic practice is that this divine forgiveness is mediated through the ministers of the Church. God did not save us "from a distance", but drew close to us when his Son took a human nature and dwelt among us. So now in confession, present now in the person of the priest, Jesus himself forgives us and grants us his mercy. Today people put the same question asked of Jesus: "who can forgive sins but God alone?" And today, Jesus tells us that - acting through his priest - "the Son of Man has authority on earth to forgive sins" (cf. *Mt* 2:7,10).

The purpose of this precept, then, is to bring us into living contact with Jesus, whose forgiveness each one of us needs. It's not that we should limit ourselves to going to confession once a year. But the power of this sacrament is so great that the Church cannot fail to require us to make use of it, at least every so often. Here the specific value of the precept shines out. Coming to confession is difficult; it can be embarrassing. We put it off, missing out on a unique and indeed essential element of our faith. So, the precept calls us, gently, out of our slumbers. It gives us a minimum which speaks to our better instincts and leads us to fulfil the call to conversion which, in truth, should never be delayed.

Another thing: making a good confession can bring us a peace of conscience and a powerful sense of relief. But it's not always like that. Sometimes - perhaps especially if we are a regular penitent - it can begin to seem routine. But the requirement that the precept places on us assures us that, whether or not it's making us feel better, it *is* doing us good.

▶ How do I make my confession?

What does the precept specifically require? It establishes that once in the year - traditionally during the Easter season - we must go to make an individual confession to a priest. Scripture and tradition give it as unavoidable that we confess each and every "grave" (or "mortal") sin that is on our conscience. These are sins committed directly against the Ten Commandments with full knowledge (we knew it was wrong at the time) and full consent (we were completely in command of ourselves when we did or thought it - or when we omitted to do something, such as going to Mass on a Sunday). If you're not sure if something is a grave sin or not, mention it anyway. Don't forget to mention any circumstances which really affect the gravity of the sin (e.g. stealing a small amount of money is different from stealing a large amount), plus, as far as you can remember, whether you did it once or more times. Note: we should always confess having broken any of the five precepts. We should prepare for the confession by making an examination of conscience: apart from the lists of questions found in some books that can help us with this, we could also read through the Ten Commandments or a list of virtues. Before making that examination we should pray to the Holy Spirit, asking him to guide us: he wants to help us more than we can imagine.

If it's a long time since you've been to confession, the best advice is: relax. You should tell the priest how long since you last came. It might be ten or twenty years, or even more, but just say so; Jesus is more patient than we think. The rite itself is very simple. After some introduction (usually you should start by making the sign of the cross, like at the start of Mass, "In the name of the Father..."), say how long it is since your last confession, then list your sins. Don't rush, be calm, and don't worry if you're struggling for the right words. When you've finished the priest may give you some advice; then he will give you a penance (some prayer or action we must do to "satisfy", through the merits of Christ, for our sins) and prompt you to make an act of contrition. This is a short formula (ask the priest if you don't know one) which openly acknowledges that we are truly sorry for our sins and sincerely resolve to avoid sin in the future. Then the priest gives us absolution, the forgiveness of sins.

▶ What should I confess, and how often?

Do we only have to say the "big ones" and not the "little ones"? Catholic teaching calls attention to another type of sin, known as "venial" or "everyday", which are the lesser type of faults most of us commit every day. To be a little irritated, to grumble at the traffic, to have an unkind thought about someone, to let our eyes wander contrary to holy purity before we catch ourselves - these things, or others like them, are the result of human weakness and habit and no one escapes them completely. The Church does not require but really encourages us to confess these sins as well, even citing particular occasions if we can remember them. To do so "helps us form our conscience, fight against evil tendencies, let ourselves be healed by Christ and progress in the life of the Spirit" (*Catechism* 1458). There is no better way to make quick progress in our Christian journey.

So is once a year enough? You would be hard pushed to find a saint - or a priest - who would recommend it. The precept, in giving us a minimum, is pointing us to the centrality of this amazing sacrament, and asking: what is right for you? Some people make their confession at both Christmas and Easter; others go to confession several times a year. To make your confession every month or six weeks is, realistically speaking, a good point of reference for practising Catholics. Pope Francis has recommended confession every two weeks; the excellent practice of weekly confession has been endorsed by many saints. Each of us needs to give thought to this question. It's good also to ask the advice of a priest about what is right for us. If we then are faithful to what we have resolved, we will never cease to be astonished by the power of God's mercy in this wonderful and life-changing sacrament.

The Third Precept:

"You shall receive the sacrament of the Eucharist at least during the Easter season"

"Truly, truly, I say to you, unless you eat the flesh of the Son of Man and drink his blood, you have no life in you" (*Jn* 6:52). These are among the strongest words of the Gospel. So much so that many of Jesus's disciples who heard them "drew back and no longer went about with him" (*Jn* 6:66). They speak to us of the reality of the Eucharistic presence of Jesus Christ under the form of bread and wine on our altars, but also of the union - the "communion" - that our Saviour wishes to have with us in this sacrament. The Holy Eucharist, as the Second Vatican Council so decisively teaches, is the "source and summit" of the Christian life. Saints and sinners down the ages bear witness that in a very unique and wonderful way God wishes to give himself to us in the Eucharistic banquet of his Son.

But why does the precept speak of receiving communion once a year, and in the Easter season? Shouldn't we receive Communion at every Mass? We know by now that the precepts speak of the minimum. But again, why does the precept give as a minimum that we receive Holy Communion "at least in the Easter season"? For many centuries up to the Middle Ages, Catholics didn't receive

Holy Communion as often as we do now - perhaps only three times a year, at Christmas, Easter and Pentecost. The reason is that in these times there was a great emphasis on the holiness of the Eucharistic Mystery, and people were afraid to approach the sacrament lightly. To ensure that people didn't stop receiving communion altogether, the Fourth Lateran Council (1215) affirmed that once a year, at Easter, was the absolute minimum for a Catholic to be united to the Lord in this sacrament. This was confirmed by the Council of Trent in 1551 and has remained in force ever since. It's at Easter that this obligation applies because the "paschal feasts [are] the origin and centre of the Christian liturgy" (*Catechism* 2042). In other words, Jesus instituted the Eucharist at the Last Supper as a memorial of his passion, and it's a pledge of our participation in his resurrection - Easter marks the time of the institution of the Mass, and the Mass directs us towards the eternal Easter of God's kingdom.

▶ An overlooked point

This third precept helps us also to register a point some-times overlooked: whilst we are encouraged to receive communion at every Mass where possible (see *Catechism* 1388) - we aren't obliged to do so, and in fact sometimes we shouldn't do so. Perhaps we'd be breaking the Eucharistic fast (at least one hour abstaining from food and drink, except water and medicine, before receiving Holy Communion); perhaps we are conscious of a serious sin we have not yet confessed. In these circumstances we can still participate prayerfully in the Mass to receive spiritual fruits. We cannot forget those who are unable by the Church's discipline to receive Holy Communion owing to their state of life (for example those in irregular marriage situations) and who rightly assist weekly at Mass in a spirit of prayer and sacrifice.

There is of course an important connection between this precept and the previous one. If someone is to receive communion only once in the year, then he or she should make their confession beforehand, so as to be sure to receive Holy Communion in a state of grace and without any sin on their conscience. But the precept perhaps raises another question in our minds: if we are receiving communion every week or every day, how often are we going to confession? Fewer people now observe the tradition of going to confession each time they go to communion, but let's notice the close connection between these two sacraments that the precepts hint at. In confession, our souls are wiped clean of the guilt of sin and we become more aware of our need of God's grace, and so we approach Holy Communion more ready to grow in that divine charity which flows unceasingly from the heart of Christ. To put it simply and directly: if we go to confession more often we will appreciate more deeply the Sacrament of the Eucharist, and, conversely, if we rarely or never go to confession there is a possibility, indeed a probability, that our communions will become routine.

▶ Where is this precept leading us?

But where is this precept leading us and what is the Church inviting us to do? Every one of us is called to ask this question for him- or herself. It is certainly a very good and today the usual practice to receive Holy Communion each Sunday and holy day. If this is your practice, keep it up! But it doesn't end there: also in daily Mass, in the midst of our working week or our family responsibilities, the Eucharistic Saviour is awaiting us with his undying love, to strengthen us with his grace. Do you need this holy strength not just once but even more times a week? There's something else too that we can't overlook: Eucharistic adoration. This practice, which has regained popularity in recent years especially among young people, focuses on the presence of Jesus in the Holy Sacrament outside the Mass, exposed on the altar in the monstrance or simply hidden in the tabernacle. Here we come to know the truth of Jesus's words: "Come to me, all who labour and are heavy laden, and I will give you rest....I am gentle and lowly in heart, and you will find rest for your souls" (*Mt* 11:28-29). Pope Benedict XVI taught that if we want to rediscover the joy of receiving Jesus in the Eucharist we need to approach him first in adoration: there, our friendship with him is nourished, it grows, and we long to be united with him in Holy Communion, not just once a year, nor even once a week, but as often as we can. Can we find time to set aside each month, or each week, to spend time with Jesus in his Eucharistic presence?

▶ The challenges we face

Let's come back to our starting point: the words of Christ and the importance, indeed necessity, of the sacramental unity with him that we achieve in the Eucharist. This applies to us individually, but it also applies to the Church as a whole. We know that we Christians face many challenges today: the faith can often seem unpopular, and many young people drift away from their Catholic roots. If the Eucharist is the "source and summit" of the Christian life then it is here, in the Mass and the presence of Jesus - Body, Blood, Soul and Divinity - that the Church must draw spiritual strength to remain faithful to her Saviour in our world. *Sitientes, sitientes!* ("Thirsting, thirsting!") St Philip Neri would say, recommending the attitude we should have to receiving our Eucharistic Lord. By prayer, devout participation in the Mass and confession, let us increase our thirst for Jesus in this sacrament, and pray that others, too, may be drawn to him in his Church.

The Fourth Precept:
"You shall observe the days of fasting and abstinence established by the Church"

The background to this precept is the idea of penance. Sometimes we call confession the "Sacrament of Penance", but here we're speaking of penance in a slightly different way: penance as a virtue. This virtue flows out of, derives from, sorrow for our sins. Penance takes the form of concrete acts (individual things we decide to do, often difficult ones) which, offered in love to God, purify us from the effects of our sins, so as to make us new in his likeness. Crucially, penance includes accepting the sufferings, even big ones, we experience in everyday life by uniting them with the sufferings of Christ on the cross. It is an act of penance to put up patiently with a headache; it is an act of penance to show love to someone we don't like.

Is penance really that important? It's striking when we read the Scriptures, both Old and New Testaments, just what a central place the idea of penance takes. God's ancient people, the Jews, frequently make atonement (acts of reconciliation) for having sinned against the Covenant by taking on themselves acts of hardship. An example is found in animal and other food sacrifices, in which part of a person's livelihood (as well as potential nourishment) is given up to God. We recall Moses fasting after he discovered that the Jews were worshipping a golden calf: "[For] forty days and forty nights…I neither ate bread or drank water, because of all the sin which you had committed, in doing what was evil in the sight of the Lord" (*Dt* 9:18). A uniquely expressive form of penance is to be found in King David's repentance for his act of adultery with Bathsheba, and his subsequent arranging of the murder of her husband. On recognising his sin, and the divine punishment that went along with it, Scripture records that David fasted and prayed (*2 S* 12:16); tradition finds in his authorship of Psalm 51 (the *Miserere*) a spirit of deep penance, in which a sacrificial offering is joined to "a broken and contrite heart", that is, to true sorrow. We think also of the famous fast of the people of Nineveh - now non-Jews, Gentiles, we note - whose king declared a fast, removing his precious robe, sitting in sackcloth and ashes, and commanding all to "cry mightily to God" (*Jon* 3:8).

▶ Christian penance

And so to the New Testament and to the orientation of Christian penance: drawing on the most noble aspects of penance from the Old Testament, it is in fact a means of communicating with God, "piercing his heart", not simply by external deeds, but as an act manifesting interior repentance and so calling down God's purifying grace. This emphasis on the inner disposition of the person is found in the Sermon on the Mount, where Jesus cautions against fasting, almsgiving or praying in order to be seen by others, but commends - indeed mandates - these practices when sincerely meant, assuring us that, looking upon our private acts of self-denial, "your Father who sees in secret will reward you." God sees our acts of penance as "cries of love" offered to his compassionate heart, and he does not fail to repay us with an outpouring of his mercy.

So much for the idea of penance. What specifically about fasting and abstinence of which this precept speaks? Right from the early days of the Church, Christians placed great importance on denying themselves food and drink as a particularly effective form of penance. Our Lord himself said of his followers: "The days will come, when the bridegroom [Jesus] is taken away from them, and then they will fast in those days" (*Lk* 5:35). Spiritual masters have shown that by frequent self-denial in this way, the body, somewhat "tamed" in its desires for food and material things, allows the spirit to rise up more easily to heavenly things: the soul becomes a little freer; our will is strengthened to choose the good; prayer becomes easier; the truths of faith are more striking. Let us tell it straight: fasting, done in a spirit of penance, motivated by the love of God, has a real spiritual effect on us which can take us by surprise!

▶ What does the precept require?

In the course of Christian history, certain times came to be particularly associated with fasting, especially the season of Lent, the period preceding Easter, in which only one meal was permitted each day, with an almost complete fast for the rest of the day. This developed into what is the current discipline, the *fasting* mentioned by this precept, which allows one full meal and one or two small snacks (or "collations") at other times of day. It applies on two days of the year only: on Ash Wednesday at the start of Lent, and at the conclusion of that season, on the day of the commemoration of the Lord's Passion, Good Friday. As a guide, if two snacks are eaten, they shouldn't add up together to more than the meal. This law applies to adult Catholics up to their fifty-ninth birthday.

Then there is the connected practice of *abstinence*. This means that no meat is eaten, including any flesh of an animal, whether red or white meat, and any kind of meat soup (but not something which merely contains a meat product - so jelly might have gelatine in it, an animal derivative, but that doesn't count). It applies to all those over fourteen years of age. Abstinence has a wider application: it applies to every single Friday of the year (unless a "solemnity" - a major feast like Christmas - happens to fall on a Friday). Whilst in many parts of the world this discipline has been relaxed somewhat on ordinary Fridays, the bishops of England and Wales determined in 2011 that the traditional application of the precept would once again come into force. According to the present discipline, therefore, Catholics in England and Wales over fourteen should not eat meat on Fridays. In other countries where the modified relaxed discipline continues, it is usually acceptable to choose any form of penance on a given Friday (be it fasting, prayer, or almsgiving), but when visiting a foreign country you should check, if possible, what the practice there is.

This recent development highlights another interesting aspect of the precepts of the Church. When this decision of the bishops was announced in 2011, it received widespread media attention. You'll probably find non-Catholic friends are interested and quizzical when they discover you don't eat meat on Fridays and want to know why. And so we try to explain that it's because of penance, and specifically associating ourselves with the cross of Jesus on the day of his death. In other words, this precept also has a missionary element: by observing it we find that our faith becomes visible. It makes the Lord Jesus visible, and the love he has for each person, the love for which he died.

The Fifth Precept:
"You shall help to provide for the needs of the Church"

The Church is indeed a divine institution, but she is also human. She exists in this world, and so she has need of the means to live and work in the world. On the one hand, if we were to think that the Church relies entirely on material things - money, buildings, etc. - we would be gravely mistaken. St Paul reminds us that in our Christian life our strength is to be found in spiritual weapons and "the armour of God", which are "not worldly but have divine power" (cf. *Ep* 6:10; *2 Co* 10:4). Yet, on the other hand, absolutely integral to the Church's mission is that she has the resources to support her work and indeed to extend it. Just a few examples show us how important this is. If just the board and lodging of a priest is expensive, think of the costs of an entire parish. Then think of the social projects that the Church operates at home and abroad. A seminary, for example, has to be built in the developing world - that's a huge undertaking. Each of these projects is "material", and yet, properly funded, each allows the Church's mission of salvation and healing to operate more freely, effectively and fully. Our giving to the Church has a direct effect on the fruitfulness of the Church's activity at home and abroad. To do so is an essential aspect of our identity as Catholic Christians.

But there's also another side to it. To give - and this can apply to charitable giving in general of course - also has an effect on us who give. Wasn't the young man in the Gospel told by Our Lord that by giving his property to the poor he would have "treasure in heaven"? Jesus adds: "Follow me". When we give with a Christian motivation, we detach ourselves from earthly possessions - which after all we are going to have to give up one day - and thereby place our hope more firmly in eternal goods, those which last for ever. And precisely in doing this, Christians find that the Lord's word "follow me" becomes easier to fulfil: putting our trust in him, letting go of some of our (probably hard-earned) money, our hearts are lightened and we become free, we become ready to hear his call and to serve him with a new-found generosity and joy.

▶ The importance of giving

St Paul offers us a further striking perspective on the importance of giving. It's he who cautions us not to rely on earthly power, but he also strongly emphasises the importance of giving materially to the Church, exhorting richer Christians to give to new, poorer communities. What are his grounds for doing so? Interestingly, they are theological: by making themselves "poor", Christians are imitating Christ in the mystery of his Incarnation, who "though he was rich, yet for your sake he became poor, so that by his poverty you might become rich" (2 Co 8:9). To give is, in other words, to imitate God himself, the giver of every gift, who is infinitely generous to his children. Do we wish to follow this divine model?

The origins of this precept - a law governing the act of giving to the community of faith - lie in the Old Testament. The Jews were obliged to give ten per cent of the fruits of their fields, and produce, to the ministers - that is the Levites and the priests - as a *tithe*. Why ten per cent? Ten was seen as the "perfect" or "complete" number (think of the Ten Commandments). So if ten stands for my complete income, whatever it may be, which can be divided into ten parts (each of ten per cent), then *one whole part or portion of my income* I give to God. This is key to understanding the precept: I have received everything I have from God, and so, each year, I return to him (in and through his Church), as a kind of sacrifice, a portion of what he has given me. This Jewish tradition teaches us that to support the Church shouldn't be an afterthought, nor simply a giving of what we have spare or left over. The Judaic observance of giving of the "first fruits" of a harvest - one closely connected to tithing, and practised in fact in a number of other religions - shows, on the contrary, that to return God's gift to God is the very first call we have on our earthly resources.

▸ How much should we give?

What, more precisely, are "the needs of the Church" of which the precept speaks? The *Code of Canon Law* helpfully expands: we give material support to the Church for "those things which are necessary for divine worship, for apostolic and charitable work and for the worthy support of its ministers" (*Code of Canon Law* 222). The first is not to be forgotten: the *worship of God* - first of all church buildings, and then for the sacred liturgy, the "summit" of the Church's life, and therefore worthy of good quality vestments, vessels, and a well maintained liturgical space. *Apostolic work* includes the whole mission of the church, including the administration of parishes, the support of poorer churches, and the proclamation of the faith. *Charitable work* (for example, the Society of St Vincent de Paul) is the service of Christ in his poor. Finally, the *ministers* of the Church, the clergy, need to be supported, because "those who proclaim the gospel should get their living by the Gospel" (*1 Co* 9:14).

How much should we give? Could the practice of tithing, giving ten per cent, still apply today? Many Christians, past and present, have kept to this ancient and biblical observance. To many, it sounds like a lot to ask. It might be a good exercise to ask: if we were to make the sacrifice of giving ten per cent to the Church, what it might say about the importance of our faith and the place the Church plays in our life? To state that everyone should give this sum would be unrealistic. Ultimately, the Church does not specify any amount but leaves it to our decision. St Paul says: "Each one must do as he has made up his mind, not reluctantly or under compulsion, for God loves a cheerful giver" (*2 Co* 9:7). Does that mean no guidance at all? As a general guide, between three and five per cent of income is typically proposed as a likely offering. But then could we give, additionally, a further five per cent to charity? (Many good causes are supported by second collections.) These figures are proposed for our reflection. If they get us thinking seriously, including about how we spend our money in general, they serve their purpose. It has been said: "A person who has love for the Church will give an appropriate offering."

▶ We are one in Christ

This precept also points to a deep truth about our unity in Christ. The Church is the Body of Christ and we are its members, as St Paul teaches. This beautiful truth, though, seems invisible: we appear as separate individuals, not linked to one another so closely as the members (the hand, the arm, etc.) are in the make-up of a human body. Of course, the unity of which St Paul speaks is a spiritual one: we are united by our Baptism, in which we share in the life of Christ and so with all those who have been joined to him in faith. And yet this spiritual union calls for continual visible expression in the day-to-day actions of our lives, so that the unity of his Body, the Church, may not be simply abstract, but concrete, meaningful and dynamic. In this way, we show clearly that we, "though many, are one body in Christ, and individually members one of another" (*Rm* 12:5). By giving to the Church, then, we are allowing her to be what she is, a communion in which we depend on one other, the weaker on the stronger, the needy on those who have.

▶ An extraordinary witness

Those familiar with the precepts from previous decades may have noticed that one, or even two, precepts, are not to be found in this booklet. The precepts in question are these: a sixth precept stated that Catholics must obey the marriage laws of the Church; a seventh, found in some books, said that we must assist the Church's work of evangelisation. Why aren't these precepts covered here? This booklet has presented the list in the modern *Catechism*, where these two additional precepts don't appear. The sixth precept, about marriage laws, is to be found in Canon Law, and its requirements continue to apply today. For Catholics, marriage is a sacrament celebrated in communion with the Church, and the Church's marriage laws reflect the fact that there is no marriage for a Catholic from which Jesus and his Church can be excluded. In order to observe what Canon Law lays down, the right course of action for a Catholic considering marriage is to speak to a priest, and, preferably, to do so as early as possible. In embracing the teachings and laws of the Church regarding marriage, even if at times they may be challenging, we place ourselves in the hands of Our Lord, who is guiding us through his Church to the fullness of love, which is the sacrifice of our lives.

▶ We are called to nothing less

The old seventh precept, regarding evangelisation, gives us a final key, in fact, for our whole review of the precepts. We saw in the case of the fourth precept how our participation in the Church's discipline - here in the (sometimes) public act of fasting and abstinence - can actually be an opportunity to be witnesses to the faith. But isn't it the same with the other precepts too? So often we hear that we are called to be witnesses to Christ in our everyday lives. But how? Of course this applies to everything we do, but the precepts, as mostly public acts which show our concrete commitment to the Church and her life, speak volumes about what is important to us and what is truly the centre of our lives. By being present at Mass every Sunday and holyday, by making a good communion, by going to confession, and by willingness to make sacrifices for the needs of the Church (the last two are not public in the same way, but those close to us may well know), we become agents of the New Evangelisation. Just think what an extraordinary witness it would be if every single Catholic in the world observed all these five precepts. We are called to nothing less.

Images

Why go to Mass?

Bishop Michael Evans

Some Catholics go to Mass simply because they have always done so, out of obligation, or because their parents, teachers or peers demand that they come. Others have either given up completely or are still searching. Relying greatly upon the new Catechism of the Catholic Church, Fr Michael Evans provides a beautiful summary of the meaning of the Mass and the powerful reasons why it holds the central position in the life of the Church and Christians. How can we love God, and our neighbour without the love of Christ?

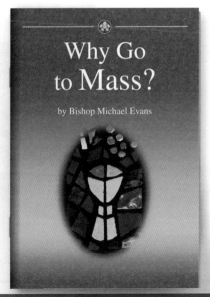

Why Go to Mass?

by Bishop Michael Evans

DO639   ISBN 978 0 85183 966 0